AF270622

Gnomes

by Grace Hansen

abdobooks.com

Published by Abdo Kids, a division of ABDO, P.O. Box 398166, Minneapolis, Minnesota 55439.
Copyright © 2024 by Abdo Consulting Group, Inc. International copyrights reserved in all countries.
No part of this book may be reproduced in any form without written permission from the publisher.
Abdo Kids Jumbo™ is a trademark and logo of Abdo Kids.

Printed in the United States of America, North Mankato, Minnesota.

102023

012024

THIS BOOK CONTAINS
RECYCLED MATERIALS

Photo Credits: Alamy, Everett Collection, Getty Images, Granger Collection, Shutterstock,
©User:ArtfulBrittani p7 / CC BY-NC-ND 3.0, ©Scott McLeod p22 / CC BY 2.0

Production Contributors: Teddy Borth, Jennie Forsberg, Grace Hansen
Design Contributors: Candice Keimig, Pakou Moua

Library of Congress Control Number: 2023937693

Publisher's Cataloging-in-Publication Data

Names: Hansen, Grace, author.

Title: Gnomes / by Grace Hansen

Description: Minneapolis, Minnesota : Abdo Kids, 2024 | Series: World of mythical beings | Includes online
    resources and index.

Identifiers: ISBN 9781098268589 (lib. bdg.) | ISBN 9781098269289 (ebook) | ISBN 9781098269630
    (Read-to-Me ebook)

Subjects: LCSH: Gnomes--Juvenile literature. | Mythical animals--Juvenile literature. | Folklore--Juvenile
    literature. | Legends--Juvenile literature.

Classification: DDC 398.2454--dc23

Table of Contents

The Myth of the Gnome

Gnomes are small, magical creatures. They have been part of human **folklore** for hundreds of years.

Early Gnomes

In the 1500s, the Latin word *gnomus* was first used in a book by **Paracelsus**. He described a *gnomus* as a small, brave creature that lived underground. It was invisible to humans and closely tied to the earth.

Paracelsus

In other early stories, gnome-like creatures were ugly. They also lived underground. They had magical powers and guarded **mines** and treasures.

Over time, stories about gnomes spread throughout Europe and the Americas. How gnomes looked changed from place to place. But they were almost always tied to nature.

In Gardens and Beyond

In the mid-1800s, statues called garden gnomes became very popular in Germany. It was believed that they came to life at night to care for gardens. At dawn, they turned back to stone.

Gnomes soon appeared in **fantasy fiction** books. L. Frank Baum described gnomes as mean and ugly in the Oz books. In C.S. Lewis' *The Chronicles of Narnia*, Earthmen, or gnomes, come in all shapes and sizes.

Disney's *Snow White and the Seven Dwarfs* debuted in 1937. It features small, bearded men with pointed hats. They work hard every day mining for jewels.

Gnomes Today

Today, gnomes mainly resemble
the beloved characters from the
Disney film. Garden gnomes still
adorn yards around the world.

Gnomes are popular in
literature, movies, and
television. They continue to
remind us of the wonder and
magic of the natural world.

More Gnomes!

Elwood
Ames, Iowa

- World's tallest concrete gnome
- Stands 15 feet (4.6 m) tall
- Weighs 3,500 pounds (1,600 kg)

Gnomeo
Gnomeo & Juliet

- Gnomeo is a garden gnome who falls in love with Juliet, another garden gnome
- Gnomeo and Juliet come from competing families who each have their own garden to care for

Papa Smurf
The Smurfs

- The oldest Smurf and the leader of all the Smurfs
- Lives in a village located in the middle of a deep forest that no human can find on their own
- Skilled in making magical potions and spells

Glossary

adorn – to add beauty to or decorate.

debuted – presented to the public for the first time.

fantasy fiction – a type of story or literature that is set in a magical world.

folklore – the stories and ways of a group of people from a certain place or country.

mine – a deep hole or holes made in the earth. Minerals such as gold, coal, or precious stones are dug out of mines; to dig in the earth for minerals.

Paracelsus – a Swiss doctor, alchemist, and thinker, who lived from 1493 to 1541.

Index

Visit **abdokids.com** to access crafts, games, videos, and more!

Use Abdo Kids code **WGK8589** or scan this QR code!